GRADED ROCK GUITAR SONGS

8 ROCK CLASSICS CAREFULLY ARRANGED FOR INTERMEDIATE LEVEL GUITARISTS

CONTENTS

PLAYBACK+
Speed • Pitch • Balance • Loop

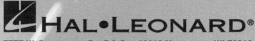

To access audio visit:
www.halleonard.com/mylibrary

8544-1928-5044-5550

ISBN 978-1-4584-0917-1

HAL•LEONARD®
7777 W. BLUEMOUND RD. P.O. BOX 13819 MILWAUKEE, WI 53213

Visit Hal Leonard Online at
www.halleonard.com

INTRODUCTION

This book contains arrangements of eight classic rock songs – each specially arranged to make them technically accessible for intermediate level guitar players, while preserving the authenticity of the original song. A recording of each song is provided, which includes the vocal line played quietly on guitar to serve as a guide. A backing track is also provided for each song, for you to play along to.

The songs were arranged by Merv Young and Tony Skinner, Senior Guitar Examiners from Registry of Guitar Tutors (RGT), and have been designed to reflect the exact requirements of the RGT's Grades 4 to 5 exams in rock guitar playing.

About RGT

RGT, established in the UK in 1992, is the world's largest organization of guitar teachers. In conjunction with its partner London College of Music (established 1887), RGT provides internationally-recognized exams in rock guitar, electric guitar, acoustic guitar, jazz guitar, bass guitar, classical guitar and popular music theory. Exams start at beginner level and progress to Diploma level for professional players and teachers. RGT exams are held in over 30 countries, including North America.

Benefits of Taking an RGT Exam

- Gain a useful and internationally recognized qualification.
- Find out, via a reliable and independent assessment, what standard your playing is.
- Achieve your playing potential by setting yourself a clear target to aspire to.
- Preparing for the exam will help you develop all aspects of your playing in a structured way – increasing your knowledge of guitar techniques and music theory.

To download a free information booklet about RGT exams, visit the RGT website:
www.RGT.org.

PERFORMANCE TIPS

Layla – Derek and the Dominos

The RGT arrangement of this piece is in the original key of D minor. There are several different guitar parts on the original artist's version of this track, so follow the notation carefully to ensure your performance is accurate to this arrangement. The opening sixteenth note phrase is played using hammer-ons and pull-offs and needs to be played smoothly and fluently so the rhythm is accurate and even. This riff is then played 2 octaves higher, starting at the 10th fret on the B string. Listen to the recorded track carefully to ensure the longer notes are all allowed to ring out for their full value.

The chords featured in the verse are performed using a variety of different techniques. The first C#m chord is strummed for its full value whereas the remaining three C#m chords in that measure should be cut short to produce a clipped sound. The dampened F#m7 chord is performed by resting the fingers of the fretting hand gently against the strings while strumming.

The chorus features a return of the main riff that appeared in the introduction and is repeated several times.

All Along the Watchtower – The Jimi Hendrix Experience

The introduction starts with a chordal riff before switching to a short lead solo. String bends dominate this introduction solo, so care needs to be taken to ensure the pitch of the string bends is accurate.

The verse features a simplified version of the chord-based fills that occur in the original version of the song. The fills are played using a combination of a hammer-on followed by a pull-off. The instrumental section that follows features the same chords as the verse but with a more rhythmic style of playing, including some damped strums.

The final verses again use the same chord progression, but with a variation on the playing style. The guitar solo in the outro includes a series of repeated unison string bends that move up the guitar neck. Ensure that the pitch of each string bend matches the pitch of the fretted note on the high E string.

Sweet Home Alabama – Lynyrd Skynyrd

Listen carefully to the demonstration track to help capture the distinctive rhythm that is used in the introduction. The fills that occur after the G major chords in the introduction are tricky to execute at first, so practice these separately to ensure the notes are played smoothly and fluently.

The chords in the verse have a clipped feel on the bass notes; rest your picking hand gently against the strings to cut the notes on the open strings short, or release the pressure slightly with your fretting hand if the note is not an open string.

The instrumental section that follows the verse contains a number of slides and hammer-ons that lend fluidity to the phrases. Make sure that the rhythm of the notes is being played correctly here when employing these techniques.

The chorus incorporates a series of short riffs that enhance the accompaniment chords. These riffs are interspersed midway by a repetitive sixteenth note phrase that uses flowing hammer-ons.

Walk This Way – Aerosmith

The introduction riff features sixteenth notes and may require some practice in order to play them at the tempo indicated. Take care to observe the rests that also occur in this introduction; bring your picking hand against the strings to silence them cleanly.

The verse riff contains a C5 power chord followed by a four-note phrase that draws on the rhythmic feel of the original Aerosmith recording. There are a number of fingering options available here as you switch from the power chord to the four-note phrase, so try to adopt a fingering approach that allows this change to be performed fluently. When the introduction riff returns in the latter part of the verse make sure to damp the notes on the low E string where marked by resting your fretting hand against the string while picking the notated rhythm. Also, notice the subtle variation in timing between the riff in the introduction and how it is played in the verse.

The chorus includes a repeated double-note lick with a slight string bend on the B string at the 4th fret. Take care here to ensure that only the B string is slightly bent up; don't bend the 5th fret note on the top E string.

The coda incorporates a variation on the introduction riff, switching between starting on the low E and A strings. Practice this slowly at first and build up the speed gradually.

The Boys Are Back in Town – Thin Lizzy

Instead of the key of A♭ major used in the original Thin Lizzy recording, the RGT arrangement of this track has been transposed to the key of A major. The riff that occurs in the introduction includes palm-muting on some of the single notes, so practice this carefully to ensure that this technique is applied only to the appropriate notes.

In the verse the chord changes occur fairly quickly and care needs to be taken so that all the chords ring out clearly for their full rhythmic value. Also, note that the chord changes in both the verse and chorus occur slightly ahead of the beat. Listen to the recorded track carefully here so that you are familiar with how these sections should sound.

The bridge section starts with a triplet pattern played across the Dsus4 and D chords. This triplet rhythm adds a sense of excitement and movement but can be tricky to play at speed, so be prepared to practice these two bars separately.

The coda moves through the chorus power chords to a short instrumental section before finishing with the main harmony riff repeated four times.

Sweet Child o' Mine – Guns N' Roses

The RGT arrangement of this track is in the key of D major instead of the key of D♭ major used in the original Guns N' Roses recording. The introduction is played with continuous eighth notes, so take care to ensure the rhythm is even throughout. Repeating this riff accurately is tricky at first so practice it slowly and carefully to adopt a fingering approach that allows for a smooth transition between the notes. You may find the notes "bleed" into each other, especially if performing this introduction with a distorted guitar sound.

The move to open position for the start of the verse is fairly quick so make sure you're ready for this at the end of the introduction. For the arpeggio figure that plays through the verses, try to ensure that the notes ring into each other as indicated in the notation and on the recorded track.

The chorus features some dampened power chords. These are performed by resting the fingers of the fretting hand gently against the strings while strumming.

For the two solos that follow the chorus, listen to the recorded track carefully while following the notation so that you are familiar with how they should sound. The second solo is an abridged version of the guitar solo featured in the original version of the song.

Under the Bridge – Red Hot Chili Peppers

When playing the introduction, listen to the click on the backing track carefully to ensure the rhythm is performed accurately. You may wish to play this section with your picking hand thumb and fingers, or with a pick and fingers. Either method will be effective, so experiment to adopt an approach that is comfortable for you.

Since the introduction is played at a slower tempo than the remainder of the song, the click that comes in for the start of the verse is slightly faster. Follow this click carefully on the backing track so you are ready to come in on time with the E chord that starts the verse. To reflect the style of the original recording, the note on the top E string may be omitted on some of the verse chords to facilitate the chord changes. For instance, on the demonstration track the note on fret 7 of the top E string is deliberately not sounded when playing the E chords that occur.

The verse that comes in after the E major 7th chord features some variations including short fills around the B chord and a chord hammer-on.

In the chorus some care is needed to ensure that only the E, B and G strings sound when playing the three-note B chord. The damped F♯m chord that is played in places during the chorus section includes an important percussive element.

Always with Me, Always with You – Joe Satriani

The chords in the introduction are all played using palm muting; place the side of your picking hand lightly against the strings to produce a slightly dampened sound.

For the main theme follow the notation and listen to the recorded track carefully so that the slides and rhythm are all accurately produced. The rhythm is quite complex in places, so take your time to ensure you are familiar with how this should sound.

The chords have been notated in the middle section rather than the lead guitar line that appears on the original Joe Satriani recording. As with the introduction, palm muting is used throughout this section and some practice may be required.

Theme 2, commencing after the middle section, is the main theme of the piece but this time played one octave higher. Make sure you're ready to move quickly down the fretboard to then replay the main theme in its original octave to end the piece.

Layla

Words and Music by Eric Clapton and Jim Gordon

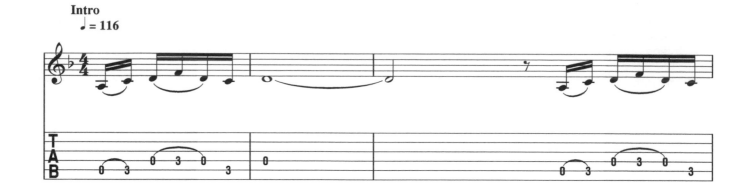

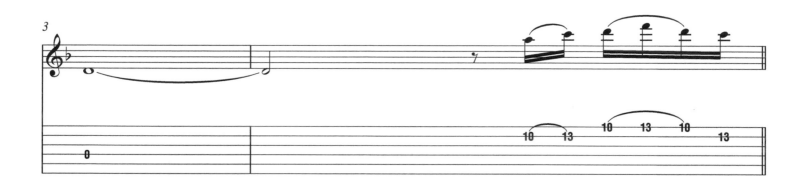

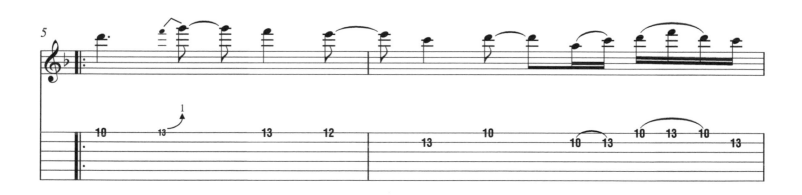

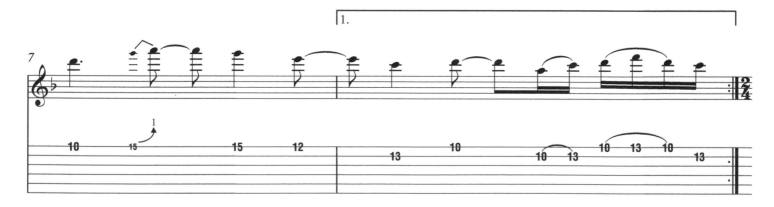

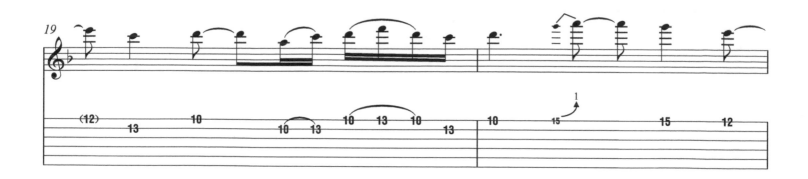

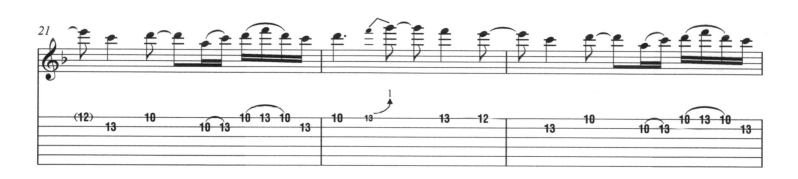

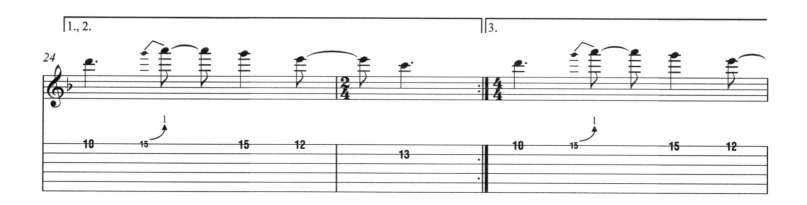

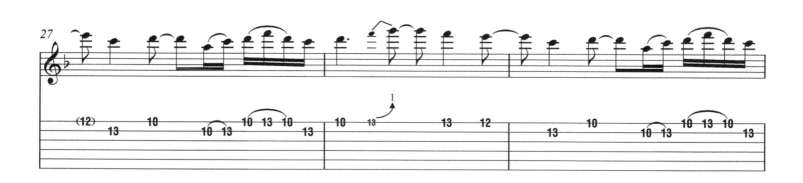

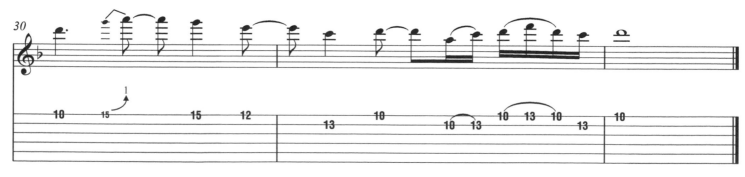

All Along the Watchtower

Words and Music by Bob Dylan

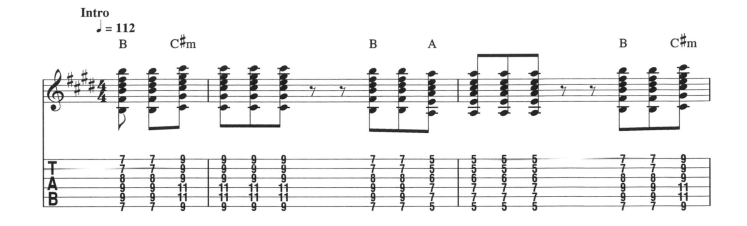

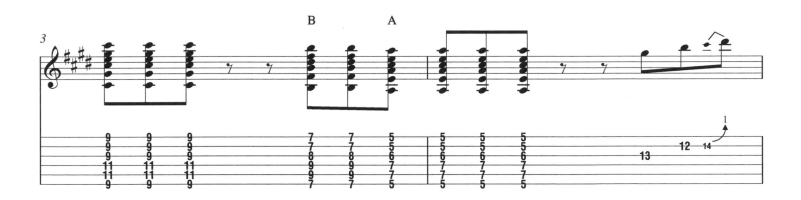

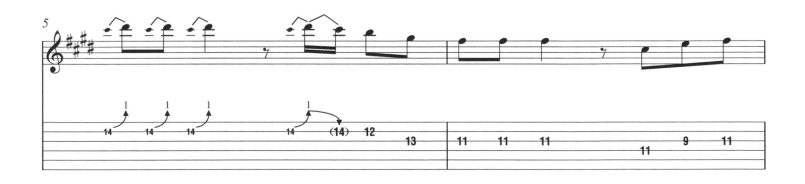

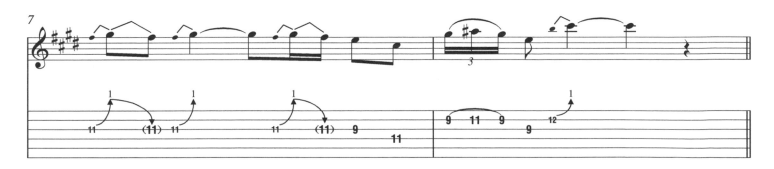

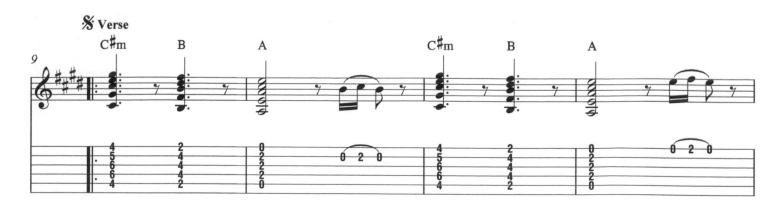

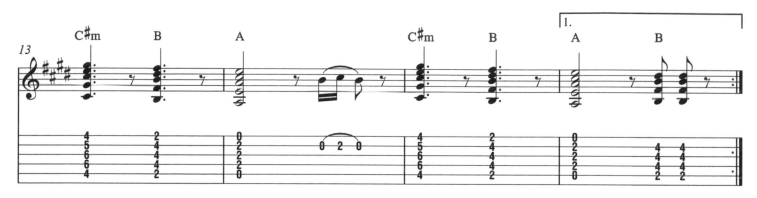

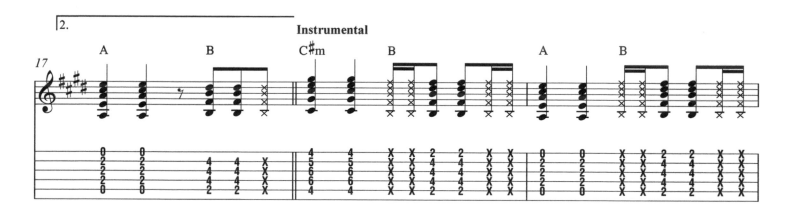

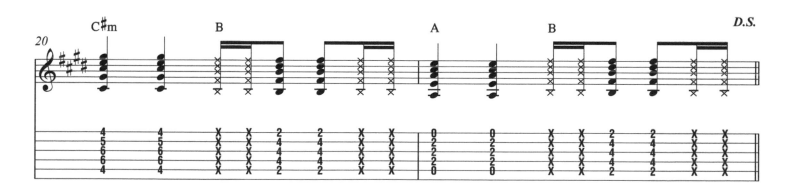

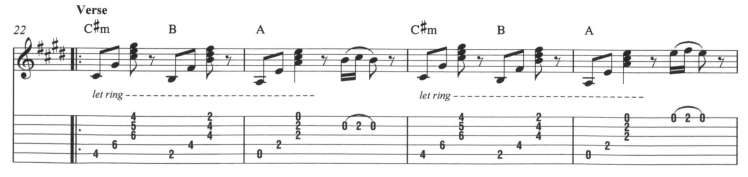

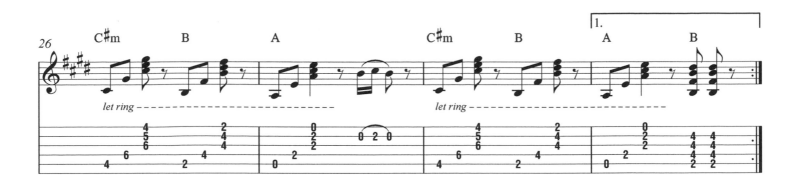

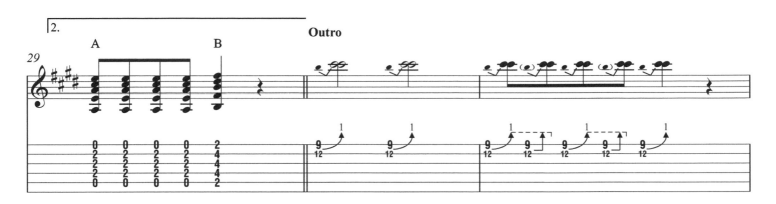

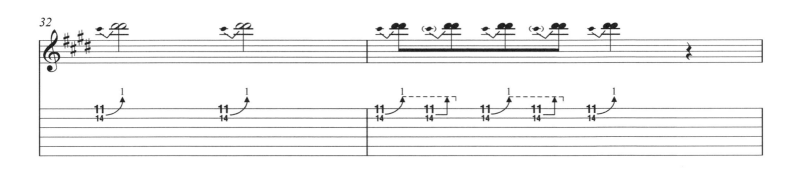

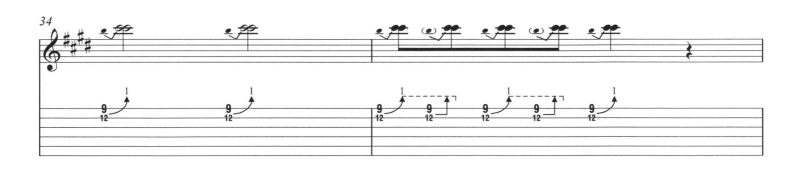

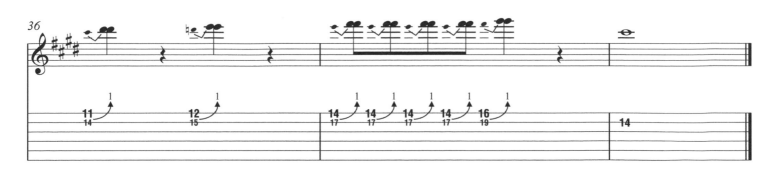

Sweet Home Alabama

Words and Music by Ronnie Van Zant, Ed King and Gary Rossington

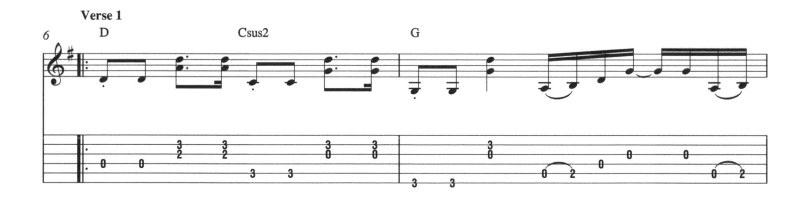

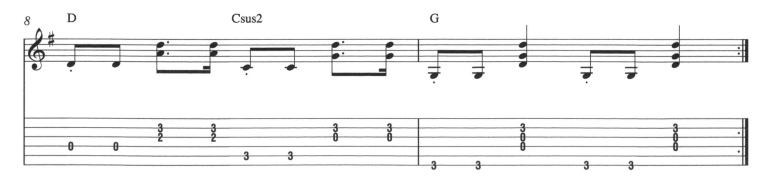

Instrumental

𝄋 **Verse 2**

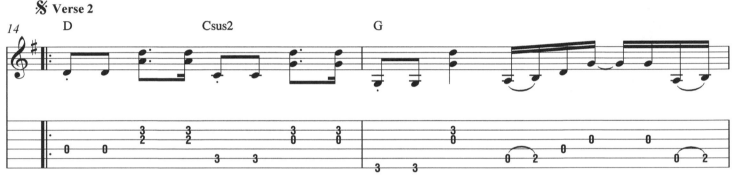

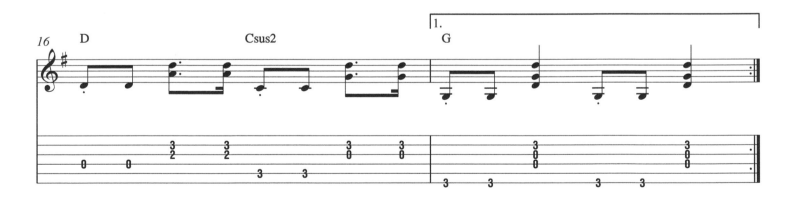

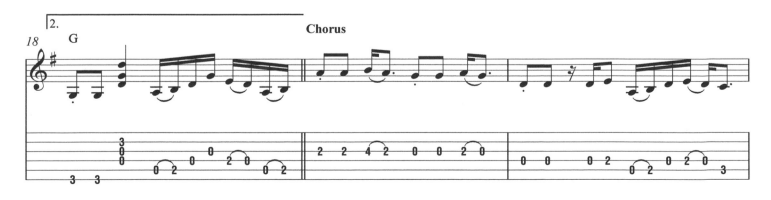

To Coda ⊕

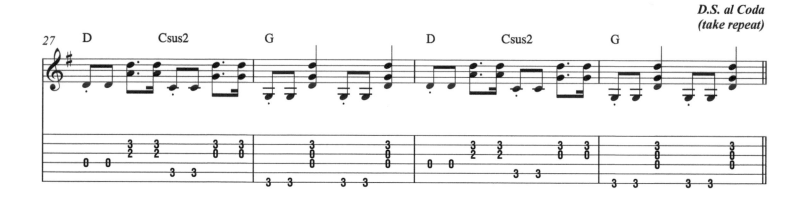

D.S. al Coda
(take repeat)

⊕ **Coda**

14

Walk This Way

Words and Music by Steven Tyler and Joe Perry

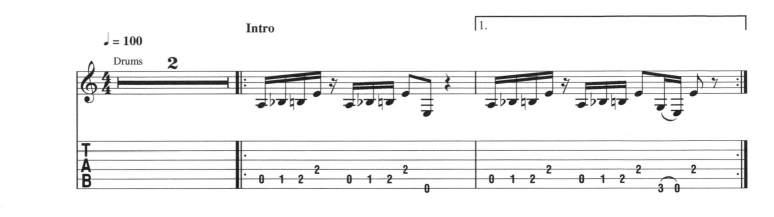

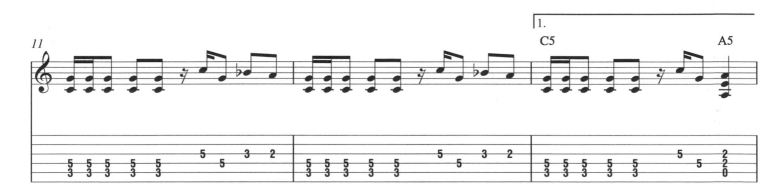

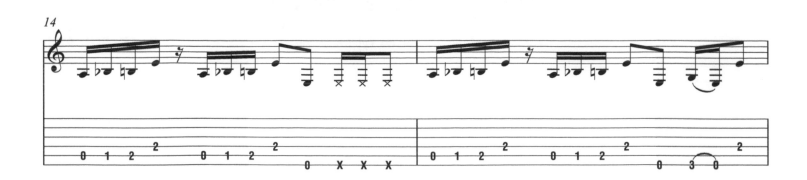

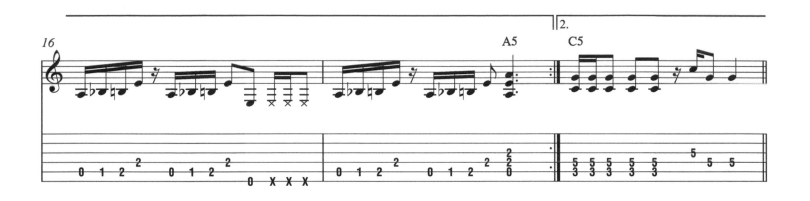

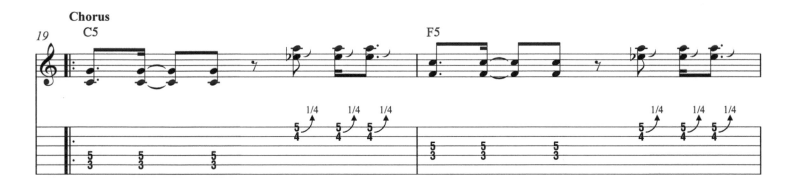

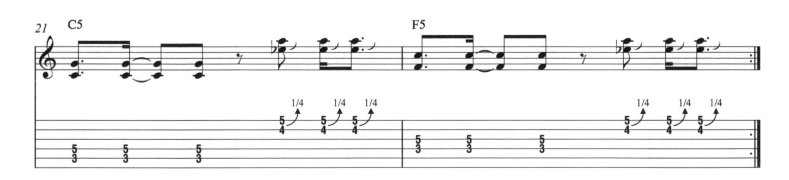

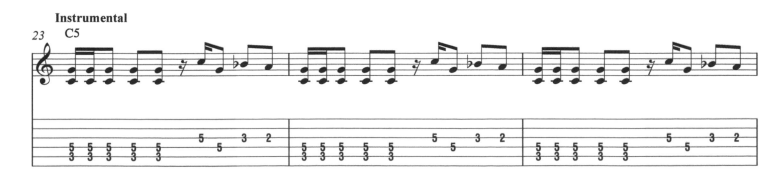

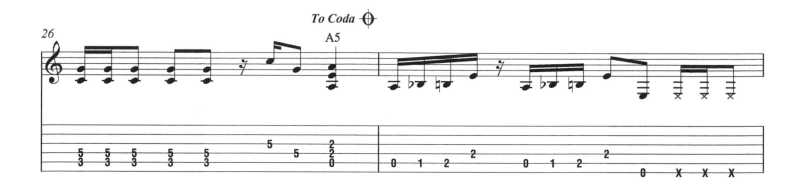

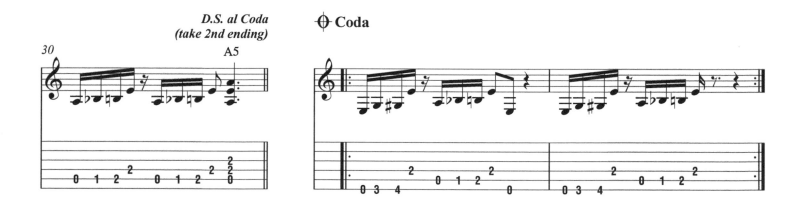

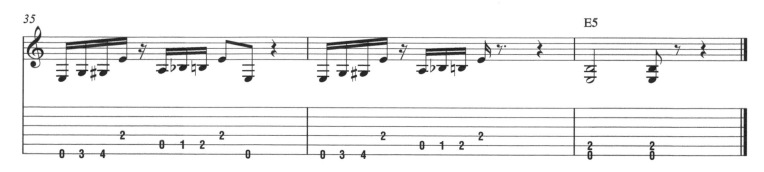

The Boys Are Back in Town

Words and Music by Philip Parris Lynott

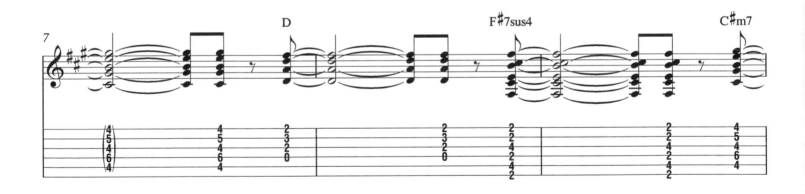

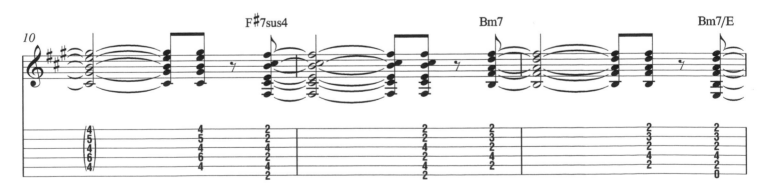

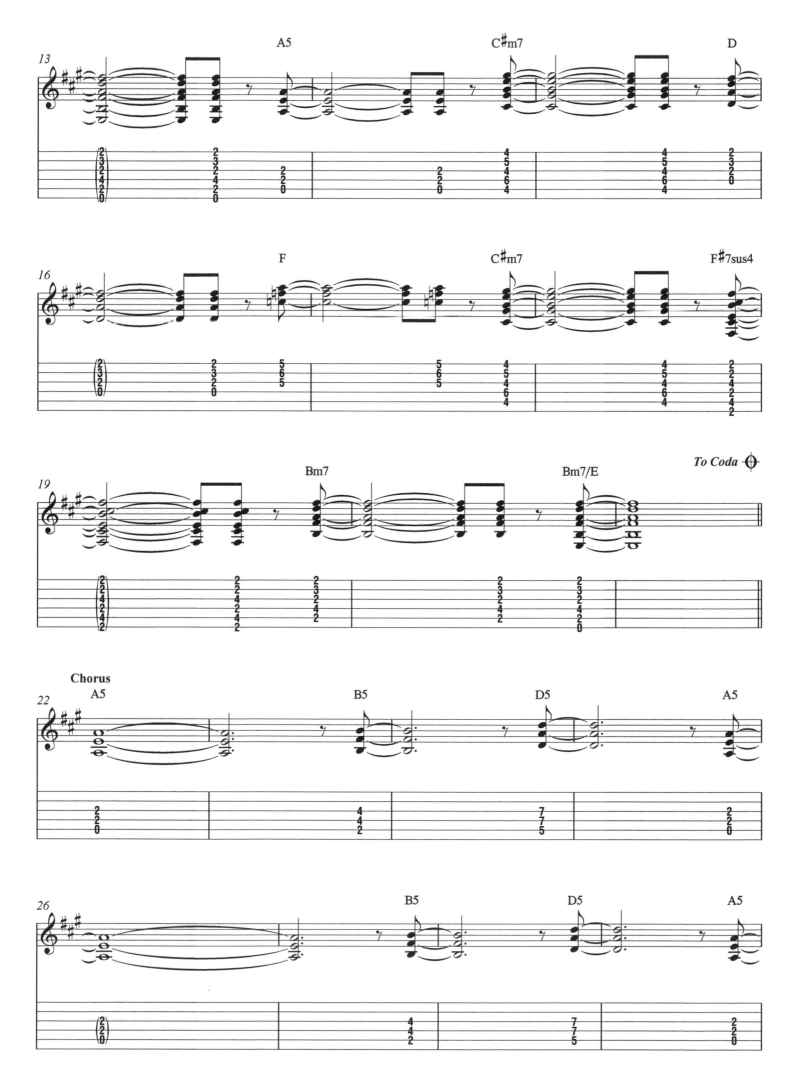

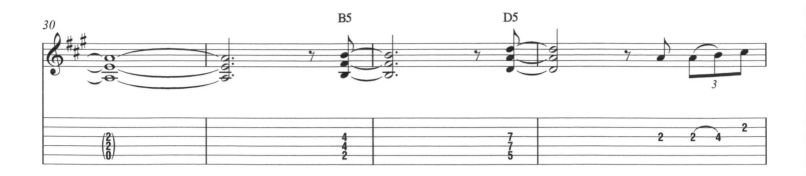

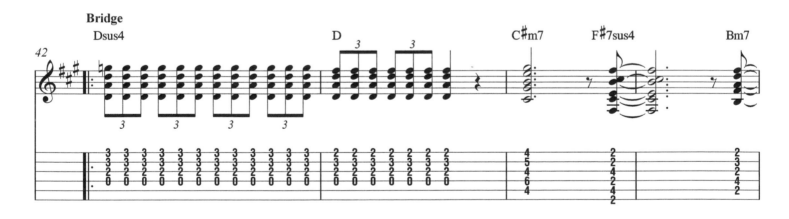

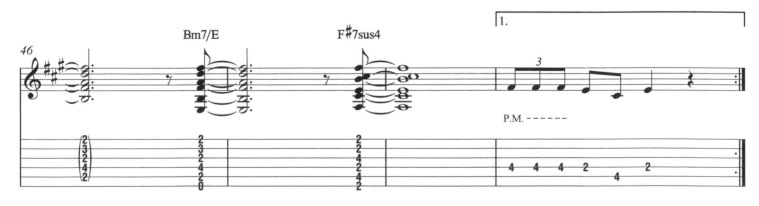

Sweet Child o' Mine

Words and Music by W. Axl Rose, Slash, Izzy Stradlin', Duff McKagan and Steven Adler

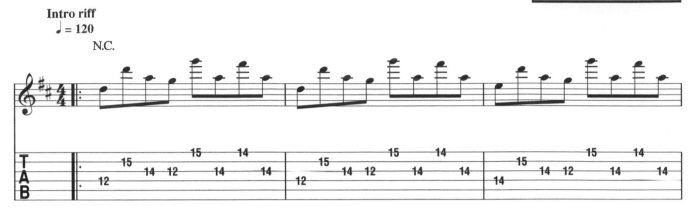

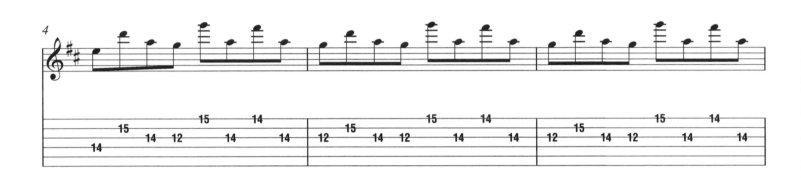

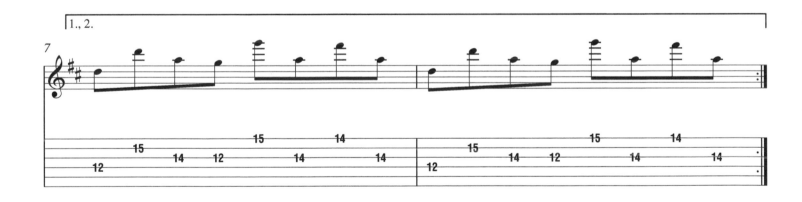

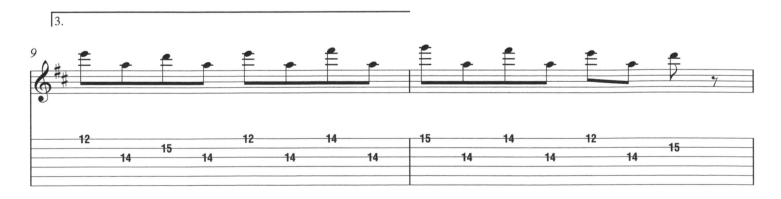

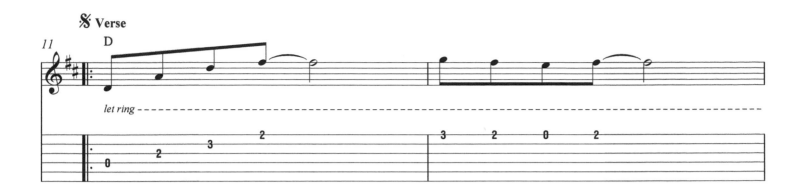

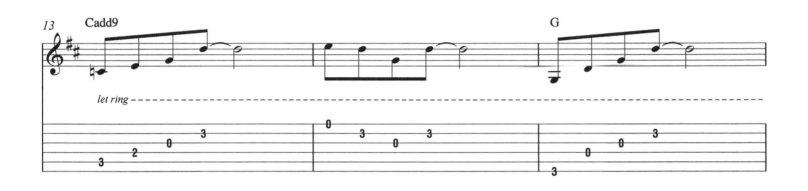

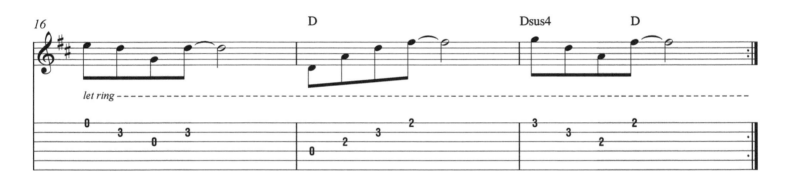

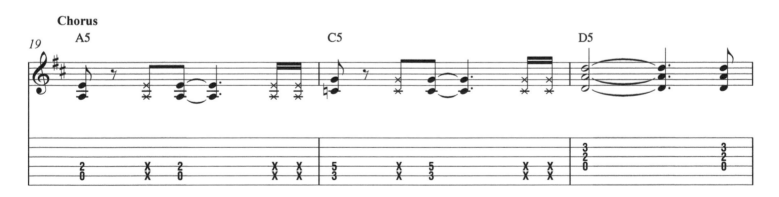

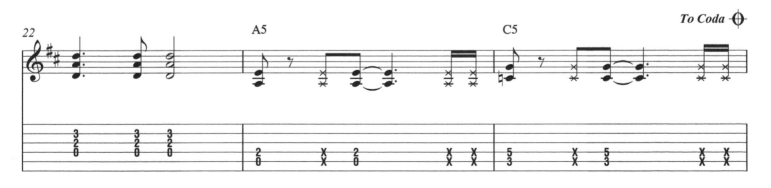

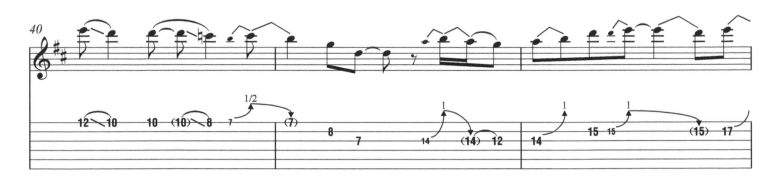

Chorus
A5

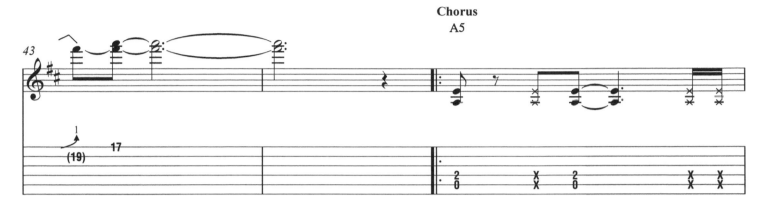

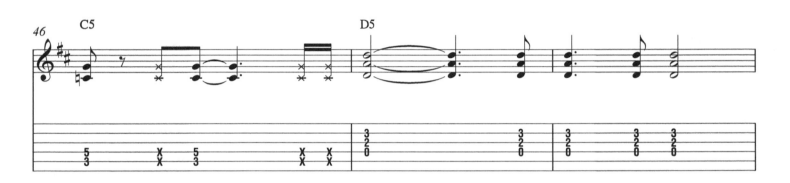

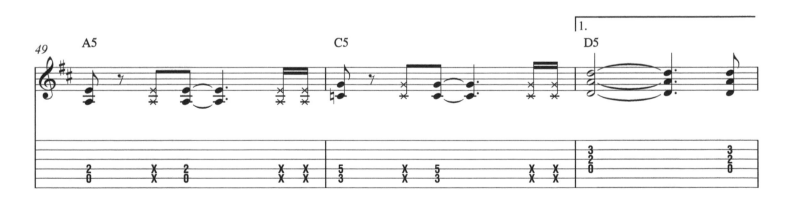

Under the Bridge

Words and Music by Anthony Kiedis, Flea, John Frusciante and Chad Smith

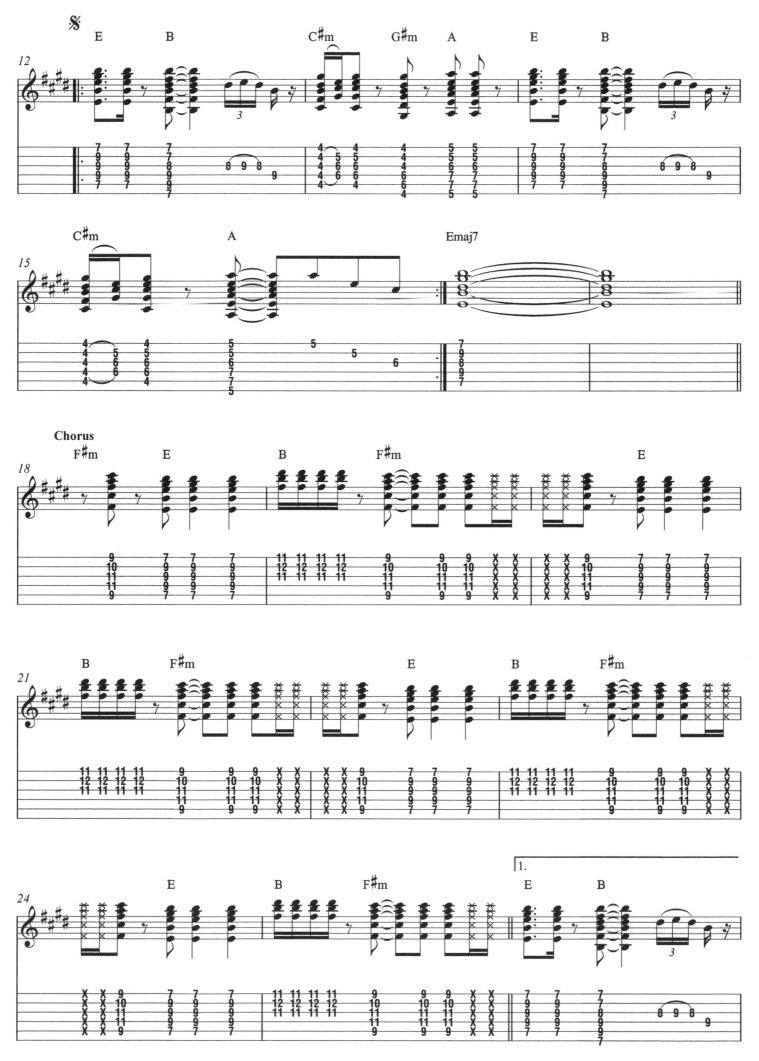

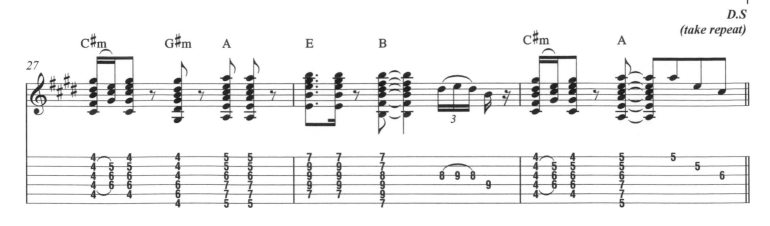

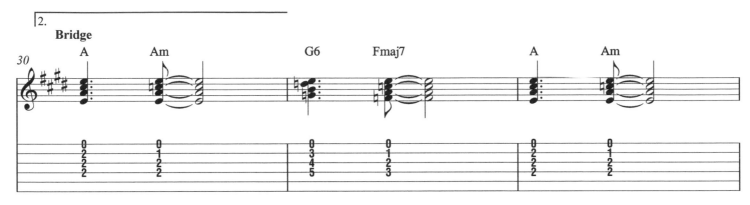

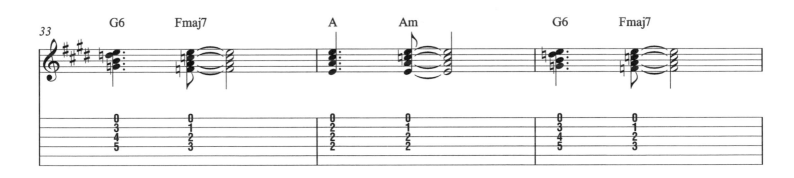

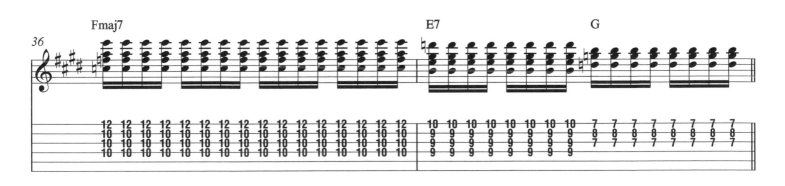

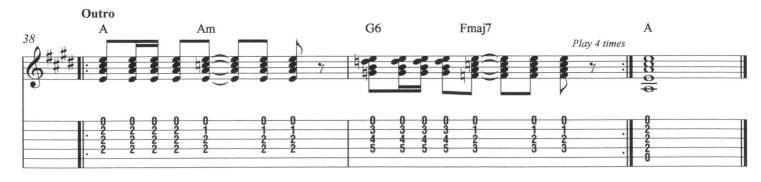

Always with Me, Always with You

By Joe Satriani

Main Theme

Middle Section

Get Better at Guitar

...with these Great Guitar Instruction Books from Hal Leonard!

101 GUITAR TIPS
INCLUDES TAB

STUFF ALL THE PROS
KNOW AND USE
by Adam St. James
This book contains invaluable guidance on everything from scales and music theory to truss rod adjustments, proper recording studio set-ups, and much more. The book also features snippets of advice from some of the most celebrated guitarists and producers in the music business, including B.B. King, Steve Vai, Joe Satriani, Warren Haynes, Laurence Juber, Pete Anderson, Tom Dowd and others, culled from the author's hundreds of interviews.
00695737 Book/Online Audio $16.99

AMAZING PHRASING
INCLUDES TAB

50 WAYS TO IMPROVE YOUR
IMPROVISATIONAL SKILLS
by Tom Kolb
This book/audio pack explores all the main components necessary for crafting well-balanced rhythmic and melodic phrases. It also explains how these phrases are put together to form cohesive solos. Many styles are covered – rock, blues, jazz, fusion, country, Latin, funk and more – and all of the concepts are backed up with musical examples. The companion audio contains 89 demos for listening, and most tracks feature full-band backing.
00695583 Book/Online Audio $19.99

BLUES YOU CAN USE – 2ND EDITION

by John Ganapes
This comprehensive source for learning blues guitar is designed to develop both your lead and rhythm playing. Includes: 21 complete solos • blues chords, progressions and riffs • turnarounds • movable scales and soloing techniques • string bending • utilizing the entire fingerboard • and more. This second edition now includes audio and video access online!
00142420 Book/Online Media...................................$19.99

FRETBOARD MASTERY
INCLUDES TAB

by Troy Stetina
Untangle the mysterious regions of the guitar fretboard and unlock your potential. *Fretboard Mastery* familiarizes you with all the shapes you need to know by applying them in real musical examples, thereby reinforcing and reaffirming your newfound knowledge. The result is a much higher level of comprehension and retention.
00695331 Book/Online Audio $19.99

FRETBOARD ROADMAPS – 2ND EDITION

ESSENTIAL GUITAR PATTERNS THAT
ALL THE PROS KNOW AND USE
by Fred Sokolow
The updated edition of this bestseller features more songs, updated lessons, and a full audio CD! Learn to play lead and rhythm anywhere on the fretboard, in any key; play a variety of lead guitar styles; play chords and progressions anywhere on the fretboard; expand your chord vocabulary; and learn to think musically – the way the pros do.
00695941 Book/CD Pack....................................$14.95

GUITAR AEROBICS
INCLUDES TAB

A 52-WEEK, ONE-LICK-
PER-DAY WORKOUT PROGRAM
FOR DEVELOPING, IMPROVING &
MAINTAINING GUITAR TECHNIQUE
by Troy Nelson
From the former editor of *Guitar One* magazine, here is a daily dose of vitamins to keep your chops fine tuned! Musical styles include rock, blues, jazz, metal, country, and funk. Techniques taught include alternate picking, arpeggios, sweep picking, string skipping, legato, string bending, and rhythm guitar. These exercises will increase speed, and improve dexterity and pick- and fret-hand accuracy. The accompanying audio includes all 365 workout licks plus play-along grooves in every style at eight different metronome settings.
00695946 Book/Online Audio $19.99

GUITAR CLUES
INCLUDES TAB

OPERATION PENTATONIC
by Greg Koch
Join renowned guitar master Greg Koch as he clues you in to a wide variety of fun and valuable pentatonic scale applications. Whether you're new to improvising or have been doing it for a while, this book/CD pack will provide loads of delicious licks and tricks that you can use right away, from volume swells and chicken pickin' to intervallic and chordal ideas. The CD includes 65 demo and play-along tracks.
00695827 Book/CD Pack.....................................$19.95

INTRODUCTION TO GUITAR TONE & EFFECTS

by David M. Brewster
This book/CD pack teaches the basics of guitar tones and effects, with audio examples on CD. Readers will learn about: overdrive, distortion and fuzz • using equalizers • modulation effects • reverb and delay • multi-effect processors • and more.
00695766 Book/CD Pack.....................................$14.99

PICTURE CHORD ENCYCLOPEDIA

This comprehensive guitar chord resource for all playing styles and levels features five voicings of 44 chord qualities for all twelve keys – 2,640 chords in all! For each, there is a clearly illustrated chord frame, as well as *an actual photo* of the chord being played! Includes info on basic fingering principles, open chords and barre chords, partial chords and broken-set forms, and more.
00695224..$19.95

SCALE CHORD RELATIONSHIPS
INCLUDES TAB

by Michael Mueller & Jeff Schroedl
This book teaches players how to determine which scales to play with which chords, so guitarists will never have to fear chord changes again! This book/audio pack explains how to: recognize keys • analyze chord progressions • use the modes • play over nondiatonic harmony • use harmonic and melodic minor scales • use symmetrical scales such as chromatic, whole-tone and diminished scales • incorporate exotic scales such as Hungarian major and Gypsy minor • and much more!
00695563 Book/Online Audio $14.99

SPEED MECHANICS FOR LEAD GUITAR
INCLUDES TAB

Take your playing to the stratosphere with the most advanced lead book by this proven heavy metal author. *Speed Mechanics* is the ultimate technique book for developing the kind of speed and precision in today's explosive playing styles. Learn the fastest ways to achieve speed and control, secrets to make your practice time really count, and how to open your ears and make your musical ideas more solid and tangible. Packed with over 200 vicious exercises including Troy's scorching version of "Flight of the Bumblebee." Music and examples demonstrated on the accompanying online audio.
00699323 Book/Online Audio $19.99

TOTAL ROCK GUITAR
INCLUDES TAB

A COMPLETE GUIDE
TO LEARNING ROCK GUITAR
by Troy Stetina
This unique and comprehensive source for learning rock guitar is designed to develop both lead and rhythm playing. It covers: getting a tone that rocks • open chords, power chords and barre chords • riffs, scales and licks • string bending, strumming, palm muting, harmonics and alternate picking • all rock styles • and much more. The examples are in standard notation with chord grids and tab, and the audio includes full-band backing for all 22 songs.
00695246 Book/Online Audio $19.99